...ly quite new ... — ...

...ful, and ...

...some oral precision. ...

...how your poetry has ...

...me you wanted to New ...

...t be in the car.

...'ll be curious to see the ...

...project Newsletter with ...

...my book of essays if yo...

...to have a copy. It's ...

...the reviewer would think ...

...language poet, since I spe...

...ment of some compla...

...poets.

UNDER THE WORLD

Carolyn Steinhoff

he woke up

... *even a moderately competent stratigrapher will, at the distance of a hundred million years or so, be able to tell that something extraordinary happened in the moment in time that counts for us today. This is the case even though a hundred million years from now, all that we consider to be the great works of man—the sculptures and the libraries, the monuments and the museums, the cities and the factories—will be compressed into a layer of sediment not much thicker than a cigarette paper.*

—ELIZABETH KOLBERT

Published by Nauset Press
nausetpress.com

Front cover design: Chloe Steinhoff-Smith
Cover painting, *Devonian Dawn*: Kristen V. H. Wyckoff
Frontispiece drawing, *Subway Sleeper*: Phoebe Steinhoff-Smith
Interior design: Nauset Press
End papers: letters to Carolyn Steinhoff from
John Koethe (*front*) and Franz Wright (*back*), by permission

NAUSET
PRESS
New York

ISBN-13: 978-0990715429

Grateful acknowledgment is made to the publications and websites in
which some of these poems first appeared.

Emerge Literary Journal "Right Now"
Dark Matter "Open Windows"
Poetry in Performance (Anthology) "Like a Boat," "The Taking Back"
House Organ "Let My Love Fall Over You"
O Sweet Flowery Roses "In My Bath"
Medusa's Kitchen "Eastern Quake: 5.8, 8/23/11"; "Don't Forget the
Infrastructure"; "Day of the Garden, Night of the Moon";
"Bottles of My Secrets"; "Body of Our Day"
Rogue Scholar "Barcelona"
And Then "Harvest Moon"
The Cape Rock "The Petal, the Air" in a previous version
titled "The Songbird, the Petal"

To my most beloved

Phoebe & Chloe
and Terrence

and to Mary

CONTENTS

On the Beach in Oregon

Far and small, the funny black shapes of pelicans passed,
always from north to south. Fifty, maybe sixty at a time,
always in perfect lines, beat their wings inches above the surface
of the silver and pink freezing Pacific. Then as if on some cue–
maybe some fish were moving–they plunged soundlessly,
first the lead bird then the next and the next,
until the line was gone without a trace.
The sky had its clouds. The waves kept up their rhythm.
And then farther south, shape after black shape,
bird by bird they emerged, their line still straight
and broken as time, wings still flapping.
Lead bird first, last bird last, they skimmed the sea,
went in again, came out, went in, came out,
into the night and the rain that were hurrying to overtake us.

The Day

The day my vein opened
and my bitter legacy ran out,
the sun slid
between clouds of salt and tears;
the moon in its icy sweetness bent close.
New York's birds raced
north along the streets,
like busses coming. Like trains.
Trees dug in their branches,
held their roots out
to be kissed. The sea rose,
took up its bed,
and walked.

And the Helloes and Goodbyes Are Never Stilled

And the helloes and goodbyes are never stilled; // They stay in the foreground and look back on it.
—JOHN ASHBERY

You came in to a place in which starlings flourish
and you'll go out from it, in which people sleep
on the cement, children dash shouting in and out
and dishes are dirty, in which little black figures
crisscross against the light in the distance;
a cloud like a fish spine races to the south
under others that are higher and more round.
As long as you are here,
the question of what your old father suspects in you
sits like something in a wrapper, pushed to the back of the cabinet.
Is it your fear of the family members
whose conversations burned
through dinner and lit the dark, who brushed their teeth
in the same house as you a thousand nights?
Your dreams about the strangers who scream at their girlfriends
and leave their dogs to bark on the foreign side of your walls?
The smell of their bodies does not pervade your sheets,
their papers and barrettes don't litter your desk
after they've moved away. Sometimes there's nothing else that can happen
but for the shells of remembrances ground to sand
to blow over you and cover you. Sometimes there is no information
waiting to be discovered and unwrapped,
only a scene replaying, in which a net of laughing fondness
catches up the friends in the room but not you.
Where the gatekeeper shakes his head
at your stammering attempts to speak,
his gaze turning your words to stone.
Drivers and passengers passing you brush you
with the music of the home that's lost to them,
of a country you haven't been to or learned about.

Don't Forget the Infrastructure

One day months ago, at the corner in front of the bank
at Church and McDonald Avenues,
a dirtpit apeared. Around and between corroded pipes
big enough for someone to live in,
men in orange hard-hats and neon vests
were busy working. A fence of orange plastic netting
stapled to plywood posts, draped with CAUTION tape,
was all that protected them from the public's gaze.
Today the fence has vanished. The sidewalk is as it was,
except the cement is clean and raw, not seasoned with spit,
urine, blood, vomit, bags, leaflets or footprints.
The new white PVC pipe sections we saw the men installing
are gone from our minds. The new surface's only opening
is one perfectly circular manhole. Its cover lies next to it
shiny as a huge dime. The last hard-hatted men
stand around it, looking down into it.

Drop from Above

A fantasy girl stumbling along
inside her body, alive in her own
or someone's mind, finds herself,
if not where she was going, then somewhere,
in a careworn room or studio maybe,
or in some life or other,
behind a careworn face
that a handful of genuine kisses could revamp,
should they be located,
while the versions of the truth that are available
are spread out on a dresser like perfumes. Should a love-object
select the truth her mind holds itself to
like cold hands to a fire,
she could hold down complaints, she feels,
a job, tears that well up, rebellions;
should the girl find emotions,
herself suddenly in a thicket,
on some street suddenly
in the thick of a life
of features not her own,
that someone found
in the trash and brushed off and assigned to her,
she could believe in her Self
the way a child who believes in the dream creature
wills himself to wake up. Should a kiss
strike her like a drop
from above, should she take the shape
and color a man desires, the white
of a sky, the endlessness
stretching beyond his sight,
the roundness of a rational world;
should she promise she'll contain him

———

when his body's spent and
he flies from it?
But artless questions—
this restlessness—shall never equal
the smells too normal to be beautiful,
a touch too beautiful to be true.

Right Now

... the emptiness turns its face to us / and whispers, / "I am not empty, I am open."
—TOMAS TRANSTRÖMER

Between one station and the next time
gapes suddenly and in my train car I'm seeing it
in its entirety as if from above.
It's some kind of mansion museum church. Rooms
open off hallways and other rooms. The alcove
that is my life, my body is breaking and from it
a new language is flying, a changed time, not crowded
with memories of everything and of the dead,
not draped with sheets of loneliness
against the damage English does.

We Are Machines

No we're not; it's a lie that we wear down.
We trade old frailties for new,
revelations for pains grown stale.
It's a dream that we see;
our eyes take as long to open
as our star is taking to burn out.
Lifetimes we take
to know what's in front of us,
what the thing is to the word for it,
word/thing, eyes/thoughts,
sidewalk/seeds falling onto it, a solo life/time
running out of it, like a rabbit,
like something scared.
Time we spend together/
loneliness we're spared.

The Sidewalk, the Air

The songbird sings for the sake of the air that language is.
The wisp of a muscled thing with its air-filled bones
has lit on a branch in the huge Brooklyn park
on its long way home, has flown in and has lit in the air
that takes the waves the orange breast and black
throat send into it, that the trill comes to exist
in and from and dissolves in.

The petal falls onto the sidewalk that is language,
that twin Japanese cherry trees reach across,
toward one another, year after year.
In three days the petal and five million other
dots of pink fleshy tissue separate
from their stems and go lightly down,
making a moist carpet the tenants,
visitors and deliverers who enter and leave
the building walk over and grind
under their shoes until it disappears.

What Kind of Day Is It?

The horizon produces one rung
of white blue-edged clouds including one large
all-blue one at the bottom of an otherwise
blue sky at nine thirty,
then below that, one all-gray row pushes out,
then more and more until at eleven the neighborhood
is grim and dark because the sky
has filled with an endless
rippled sheet of heavy gray
that only certain rays of sunlight can penetrate.
At noon a blue background
shows through a tear.

A Meteorite Streaked Across

A meteorite streaked across the sky and exploded over central Russia on Friday, raining fireballs over a vast area and causing a shock wave that smashed windows, damaged buildings and injured 1,200 people.

—REUTERS.COM

Like a poem looked to
until its truth faded I made
some substance, some
comfort from your words I don't dare
remember into a nothing-proof vest of leaves.
Then revelations burned their
trail through a day that was dark—
grammars lit up then shattered—
pushing what you wanted
me to think out
of my brain. From the scene—
habits better off
broken, glass, mementos strewn—
rise stifled cries, of creatures
small and not smart enough made to risk and be born.
Stripped by
illicit notes I fold a call to god
fallen back to earth around
my nakedness, love I thought
existed stood up
shimmering and
rustling around me, a golden grove
in a dream, branches, fallen
fruit under the trees free
for the taking.

Day of the Garden, Night of the Moon

With all the people dazed to find that time
is only a carpet of moonlight on waves,
I put into the wide sea of your body;
I should keep my eye on our one star,
because your smile is as close to me as mist,
your looking at my looking at
you the most enthralling song,
our sex our element; I'm dazzled by this
New York we kiss in, this backdrop
for the sweet-faced moon, Irish,
showing herself to us hearing too
the ghosts of failed loves saying
"Don't you want us back" into our ears,
our minds like birds in grass,
us standing upright under buds light, dark pink, white,
breaking faith-filled into the aching blue
in the garden on the one life-long day of its flowering.

Barcelona

I thought I would come to Spain for the beggars,
that I would unfold a table for them on La Rambla
and set out course after course
and that only the thieves would be invited, and you would be among them,
you who search through drawers full of other people's clothes
and rub your sticks together like two halves of a beak,
you who bend over me like a plane tree
bending over the traffic in front of the sun,
who shrivel like a hibiscus outside the arms of your wife,
your voice taken off me as I lay in my hotel in the boiling dark.
I thought when I was awake without you
in the midnight of the world, in its foreign dry beauty,
that the dead leaf groping the building would clatter over the stone street
    as you clatter
around your half real memories of girls without flinching
from the sticks and the withering eye of the sun
that covers the glassy Mediterranean with its glances,
that writes thoughts and their revisions down on the rocky edges
where the people laugh and scream in the ferocity
and tenderness of their desires.

I thought my first step down the stair
would be into a sky of artificial footholds and that my movements,
visible inside the darkened eye-level room,
would boil me until my shell opened
and I exposed my muscle to the darkness.
I thought I would appear
out of the dark like a gnat,
to bat at the window of your eyeglass lens,
because in your eye an enthralling scene was being played out,
in which I wanted to be allowed to take part.
You would be the bird that sings only at night I thought,

from that one tree in America,
only when I walk alone with my master
in dry mountains with their bald crags
in the historic center of the world.

But the darkness
completes itself and you swim into it like a white fish.
You make your hands into a new kind of eyes. You count your steps.
One bird dives after the other,
straight into the clanging that emanates from the bells
in their towers, out across the withering sea.
The soft trees obscure and protect the houses,
the churning of quietness hides itself in the sky.
The sparrows rattle their wings in it to tease us
with their proximity. Under the burning mantle
of our not thinking of one another we give our voices
like water to the strangers in their kitchens and at their fires.
The water that in August shrinks from their mouths,
in November can't be contained in its bed.

The Siren of the Future Coming

The fact of my remoteness permeates my body like metal.
Soon a cosmic something will lower a rope
and yank me so completely out of this world
it will be as if I had never been. I'll even glimpse
the love I am as starved for as I am unpracticed in,
like a redbird lighting for a moment in a green
tree and redeeming it. Who has grief not ravaged?
When I was a little girl in school, all you had to do
to be good was to fold your hands in your lap.
Today the thoughts I light and place around my apartment
blind me. I can't see myself doing I know not what,
I suppose feeling the greediness of desire through my skin,
listening transfixed, I suppose, to the siren of the future coming,
lights flashing, the red and white speeding chariot. Over the rooftops
   next door,
a cloud of sleep hovers for me. Let it draw me into it and there
will be a home with my children, full of talking and laughing and
   cooking smells.
The divide between saving and destroying will dissolve
into the picture of the world I want. I will throw my mistakes
into the air there, and shoot them to smithereens. There I'll be, fighting
   in it.
I thought I was the strongest thing alive,
because the soft butter in my skull is so complicated.
But I am a tin figure passing other tin figures I call neighbors, my girls,
   Mom,
in parallel slots, controlled as we are by something with rods from
   underneath.
Under my sleeve my watch ticks and changes.
Under my shirt my lungs pull in the silence and let it out.
From a train window last week I saw an endless lawn,
people in black clustered between rows of stones,

liquid people soaking the fleetingness of the world
in through their skins. Under my ceiling, flowers
stand at attention for a time, then hang their heads, then dry.

Bottles of My Secrets

The world seems subject to so much whipping up,
a trackless sea constituted as it is
of what everyone wants of me.
I'm so tired of tossing in it
I'm bottling my own desires up right now
in pretend glass of uniform size
in every color and shape—blue fish, brown mermaids,
yellow trees, green bathtubs, orange moons, purple sparrows—
and arranging them on my dresser, in space, or in my ribs.
Instead of leaving my efforts splintered like timbers,
a hurricane of words someone said
will make no more wreckage of second guesses
heaving in me all wrong and pointless. My purple sparrow-shaped
Deadly Night Terrors, the orange moon
labeled *My Unbearable Losses* might temporarily dissolve,
but I will form them again, no one can stop me. I love all of them,
but my favorites are the red one, *Forgetting All About Time*,
shaped like a clock with no hands, and the clear one labeled
Overwhelmingly Intense Desperate Love, shaped like me.

This Fall Should Be Memorized

A season changes color to no end, / Except the lavishing of itself in change
—WALLACE STEVENS

See why people have their secret love affairs
with Jesus and God and English
and the Big Bang? For making a world
with a Brooklyn like this in it,
with a fall like this one in 2010,
never to be seen again, for having words like
sacred, riotous, saturated, gorgeous
to call these colors, the primitive
ginkgos' primitive monochrome
the epitome of yellow, and then the gradations
from rust to scarlet to candy-apple red to
alizarin crimson to tangerine to bittersweet
orange to mahogany that are everywhere,
blendings of mauve with purple and gold turning
from lemon to aureolin on all the trees, even on single trees,
even on single leaves, tiny flat deep-red berries,
small round citrine and dark goldenrod and saffron leaves
lining low bushes' fine branches sticking up
and out and crossing each other in perfect disarray.
Pines and holly intersperse themselves freely,
resolutely dark green except for the coquelicot red
balls in their spiky leaves. I love the makers
just for this street, for these plants performing
their flamboyant ritual of dying to show us how,
undeniably a free gift for me personally to gaze at,
my intact sight undeniably a free gift to match,
my eyes and these leaves made for each other,
proof that they want me to notice,
to not be able to help giving words to
the magnificence of earth,
the phenomenon called life, called live
things, human things, to exult
that I am one.

Last

The monarch on its way over a city,
a question asked, an answer
hover above our brains
weightless as sound. This old
face in the mirror is not the one
I saw there last; these arms
alien and strange extend themselves
from my body, folding like a shell
around a grain of something,
shielding some naked privacy from the wind.
This dreamlike love I won't wake up from
blows by ceaseless as traffic.
Sliding over the streets and flowers,
where has it lifted itself up from,
this cloud of cries of the stricken,
one escaped out of my own throat?
From the sea? It sounds not human
but aching and clear as notes,
as the call of the last bird.
We hold it in us
like a breath under water.
What lasting and lustrous thing
can we make, boyfriend,
from the grain of terror that's in me,
scratching the secret
flesh of the self? A current suspends
the butterfly going home to Mexico
among the towers of New York.
Trees are all pink and white
down there for it.
Their frothed-up branches wave.

Aerial View

... into the absence of all I knew and was bound by ...
—MARK STRAND

On streets ordered as a child's gameboard
the houses of people I know are arrayed
in perfect rows.
From inside my body, mesmerized,
I look down at them
as if from a plane,
see the tiny shadow of my life running
over their rooftops, as fleeting to the inhabitants
as a premonition. I think heaven
is how cars down there turn from ants
to beetles to toys, how they become rides. How,
earthbound, one can not only see and visit
but be part of. I think heaven
is where bodies and their shadows join.

Views

Little Boy Blue / Come blow your horn / The sheep's in the meadow / The cow's in the corn / Where is the boy / Who looks after the sheep? / He's under a haystack / Fast asleep

—MOTHER GOOSE RHYME

1. *A Mother*
How is it that she,
the stranger off to the side,
in this square of shade
under this tent, here to see
the foreign boy
her daughter married then left
playing his foreign sport on this field,
how can it be that she can see the tears
wetting the faces
of the two little boys,
one about four, the other two,
that what she and all the players' wives
want to do is gather them up
while their mother talks on,
her voice louder
than the sound of their crying; how does a mother laugh
as if no one is pulling her sleeve?

2. *Neighbors*
Her attention closes like a shell
around what's there—
a fire escape;
her big-breasted neighbor she sees
through lonely tears
shake that quilt out
the window in the brick wall again;
the young couple, in their home,
that looks at TV and her;
they cover themselves
for each other. A small house,
the one tree in its back yard

a catalpa, performing its rituals,
giving its oxygen to their lungs,
its flowers to the ground between them.
It sleeps with its branches bare.
The crow on the roof across from hers
showing her the yellow Brooklyn light
thick on its black black wings.

3. *A Lake*
From a tiny handmade plane,
its pilot and three passengers—
she, her love, his boy—
see a crater between mountains,
bottomless as that place in her.
Filling it, a lake, a blue so improbable,
so sharp it pierces their eyes,
strains their belief,
etches itself
rare as mercy
into their brains.
Where is the shepherd?
Who looks after us?
she's wondering.
Will you be my blue?

Lullaby

Who wants to rush headlong
into solitary wakefulness
in a darkened city not their own?
In my dreams the forsaken don't refurbish
their store of slights; calls not returned
dwindle into the sky.
On the buildings over the water
windows glitter and proliferate.
Their glow subdues the blackness
of the night as long as it lasts.
Their tops are many colors
and strain toward space
and beckon to my train of sleep.
People, run in a silent stream
down the steps toward the well-lighted cars
that stand there waiting with their doors open
in the depths of my memory to receive you.

Under Construction

What is a bald stocky Russian
in a black leather coat doing
standing on that shallow third floor
terrace like that, as still as if he were
at home transfixed by the song
of all the time in the world behind him,
singing to him like a lover in his rooms?
What is he doing standing there,
with nothing but a lattice
of girders every which way,
full of light; what is my body doing,
pressed tightly between the world's beginning
and its end; why is he there like that
with nothing behind him
but a building that's only half built?

Safe Behind the Glass

In the building across the street
a cat preens behind glass.
"The light beyond the gate would shock you
every day with the different strangeness
of its embrace," she says to it.
"Yellow one day, harsh white the next,
it stamps hydrants and ragged pink roses
with its unpredictable qualities. Cloudshapes graze in it,
enlarge as they blow closer, impress on us
the whitened opacity and bulkiness of their vapors.
A rim of trees forms a lit-up hem
on our big darkening neighborhood.
Leaves, and birds you will never stalk,
tear from the sidewalk to space and back,
in the wicked and intense and freezing wind
that dares us to put a toe outside."
From her window, houses seem to her to buck up
under the renegade light
spreading from one roof to the next
before the shadow comes back over
their chimneys, antennae, asphalt
tiles and satellite dishes. "This will surprise you,"
she says to it, but the cat is gone.

The Body of Our Day

There, while we're force-feeding lakes, rivers and seas to the sky
 until it's so swollen with clouds,
so out of sorts and sullen that it pins us to an equally sullen, fed-up earth,
the body swims through the silence that absorbs its offerings, its wants,
 its press against space,
as primitive in the air of our time as a water bird under a river.
Words by the thousands are held in it, like breath. The art of a life
 —to bear invisibility—is a lost art.
The new big thing is to be seen.

While the ear strains for meanings only the dead remember how to convey,
while the body, trespasser at edges—of seas, of photographs, of other
 people's families—
burns to give speeches directly to someone, is parched in water, drowned
 in space,
taking to wandering theme park cities looking for a home,
while the art of today—a primordial art—is to be alive, the stylish thing is
 to have.

Though the art of our time is to get cut and bleed, though the body is a
 lovely holder of ashes,
there in their little room, like a cormorant on the surface, in an instant,
 out of nowhere,
between two who exist for each other appears ... world without end.

New York Quake: 5.8, 8/23/11

Among rocks, dirt and plants
instead of buildings, crowds and traffic,
through cold shade and hot sun,
past young velvety ferns
spreading like hands
over a lichen patch,
we climb Vroman's Nose
to a jutting shelf of stone
from where we see
that the whole Scoharie Valley
is given to Monsanto
corn. Green-blond rows
stretch up slopes and around
bends and barns and towns
in and out of our sight.
The last dark tall wild
trees allowed to stand
are uneven along the black
looping river, right bank
mirroring left, like parallel bands
of fur trim on a private
lonely wet cut. I
with my privacy,
and you, boyfriend,
with your loneliness
are content because we're touching,
and don't feel the earth shuddering.

The Eclipse

His face, and the faces of his admirers, are on this side;
hers is over there. The veil he's pulled down
between the two of them
reddens trees, clouds, buildings, even the moon.
Pictures of her litter his nights; his arms stretch
into his bedroom's reaches, they cross one over the other,
uncross; his arms extend from his sides like logs.
Light accrues behind the horizon while he lies awake,
last year's light, sticking to what once were stars.

Open Windows

Red flowers appear
like cuts in the air
of one crowded apartment.
An atheist hears those bells.
A woman in another,
as old as I'm becoming,
flings out an exhalation
like a ring an ex buries in the sea;
coughs, disconsolate sobs,
yells in accents and languages fly,
cries during sex between two
who thought they loved others or no one,
who eat up the kiss for the hunger
that stays on their lips and tongues.
Each day at six, silverware clinks
without voices—a solitary tenant?
A silent couple? A wife eating alone?
We strangers breathe in
the smell of her casserole,
which is delicious,
imagining that certain bitter taste
that could be sticking in her throat.

The Kisses of Life on Earth

Can I float without a care on top
of a bottomless world that hurts and calls to us?
The arc of heaven that encircles it
answers me by pressing its very blueness
into my eyes, by its tender deepening around the branch-ends
that deepen their new green in return saying, "I know you,"
saying to me, "You could hold yourself out
like we do"; can I believe it?
That we could not flinch
at the silent dark that comes for us,
huddled as we are on our mattress-rafts
one by one, two by two in the night-times,
replaying the hurtful scenes in dreams?
That I could hold in the feeling
I'm bursting with, as the hard buds,
the black buds say, the sorrows that freight the blood
my heart sends around and around its course?
Is aloneness—are your thoughts—really closer
than space, than my emptying city;
are those trees, your kisses, really life on earth,
raining on my lifted face
like a shower of softly falling stars?

Harvest Moon

Like a banner advertising oblivion,
trailing our train over a beach made of buildings,
the night flew with us,
as if invisible strings tied it
by its frayed edge to our last car.
With that opaque cloud curtain close behind,
we lumbered up and out from the tunnel
onto the high trestle in front of Manhattan,
into the still half-lit gray remnant
of the day that seemed to have put all of us to sleep,
even this—what was this gigantic rust-colored face
with shadows for features dwarfing Brooklyn?
We riders were given one glimpse of it
that we were too worn out to recognize or be awed by,
before our train drew the terrible, the blessèd dark forward,
blacking out everything too strange
to believe, everything in sight.

Dream City Explorer

Yesterday I entered the dream city
that the future is
to see if you and I were in it.
I found my darling girls old,
my friends now ghosts, calling to me;
I heard the air between leaves passing
like thoughts between lovers:
When we part
do you disappear from the world?
I saw days filled with fears like this
but emptier than ever,
teeming with more wishes than sparrows,
but lonely. What can I ask of you?
To convince me I exist?
To invent me?
Let's you and the new me run parallel
to the point where our lives converge,
beyond my last dream that you're missing.
Beyond my words never said.

For the Love of the Trees and You

How will I know what current you keep in you,
whispering against me even while I chatter on to you
about everything under the sun? I am too busy
talking of dust's accumulation,
of hunger and thirst, the timeliness of messages,
to read the signs naming the rivers
I catch out of the corner of my eye.
What can I make of your frowns of hurt
I don't even look up from my book in time to see,
when I'm rolling down streets of air that extend
in all directions at once, that cannot be traversed in a hurry?
When I'm exiting the invisible maze
in front of and inside of everyone,
as wildly improbable in its colors as the Northeast's
October corridors, showing that the world never suspected
we doubted its love for us? Pink and gold and purple trees
rush by our bus windows in the form of time,
each leaf an instant clinging
to the blue space we're passing through.
Road under us, buzzard turning above our heads like a dial,
earth, tell me how I'll know what up means,
what is down. The market, your estimations and affections,
the speed with which my blood flows around and around its paths?

As We Were

Through our holders of flesh
and barriers of bone his and mine,
the life inside this other
is striking, silent, striking
my cheek like a fist, the breath
of love he's holding, putting in
me is swollen, to show
that I can bear limitless things,
even our failures, to prove
that my body is open as a sky.
If I could turn my face without flinching
to that day that waits,
then these multiplying pleasures
we're being given tonight
from some infinite pure store
might not seem stolen.
If my body weren't changed
by the press of his
before he turns to the door,
to the stairs down,
my face not lit up
by his singing *Have I Told You*
Lately to me ... but it is ... so
with each breath we are born and die;
the worlds in us collide.
We'll never be as we were.

In My Bath

*... the earth's shadow into space is blood red and about eight and a
half hundred thousand miles long ...*

—KEVIN HUIZENGA

No one is witnessing me stripped
by the pressures of the job, the demands of love,
preserved whole in the center of the universe
in a hot clear casing, itself in turn squeezed
within the first layer of air pressing
against my side of my apartment walls
that hold themselves hard and upright against
the deeper air, pushing them on the other side,
between them and the walls of my building
they're parallel to, which ever so gradually
are being worn to dust by the capsule,
made half of dark, half of light, that my small earth,
anomalous as it is, covered with the living,
turns and turns to accommodate.

What To Think About?

With one daughter in Sri Lanka,
having left the other,
the younger of the two,
in the West to live,
I'm in a black sky
with a blue-white planet
above black Nebraska.
See the earth's
yellow-green patchy rash
of glowing towns.
Look at the screen
on the back of the seat in front of me—
the white line inching longer—
our progress toward New York.
If you were a river
like that one down there,
twenty years old,
looping your way
round the bends like that,
you would have better things to think about too,
than a person in a plane.
If you were a plane,
the gray-black soft nothingness
of the cloud you'd be inside
would be spare and blank like this,
like a mind without its thoughts,
like a mother without her girls.

The Taking Back

Floods above, come out of us,
meet floods below.
In some twisted synergy
between prisoner and guard,
master and slave,
sinner and God,
one sky-sea's taking the poor, the weak,
huddled in cold apartments, in cells,
under its huge black wings.
Weather canny as ravens
issues its forms in triplicate to fill out.
I am as crumpled as faded writings
among your papers, nothing but a receipt
to prove to the warden you've paid.
But for what? Have you been sold yet
on taking me back?
Love become signing on a line,
the words unrevisable,
promises taken back strewn
over the streetscape,
melting like clocks over fallen trees.
The seas we've built on,
that our bridges arch their backs over—
they want our cities.
Scramble our seasons.
Take back their lands.
I cling to words thin as sticks,
children and I, a man in love,
who wants to let go.
Pets held dear float by,
and cars, beliefs in our powers.
The one truth left us,

we wouldn't learn: nothing
is eternal. Certainly not the life in me
you take first into your hands, then
through them into your home, your blood.

What Is There

How hard can we search our own selves to see what's there,
like the horizon at the end of the sea, like a sky with three stars,
a drawer full of odds and ends—matches, a wedding ring, a cork, a broken
   watch?
Is what I uncover there love,
a geometry of emotions in the air?
Does a pure moon round and shining exist,
smiling down on us in our follies?
Or is what I come upon just you,
a dream or thought of you
standing in a space that's smarting with absence and filling it?

All the Still Still World

Since the earth and its wonders have given rise to me,
I should not keep thinking of the cloud that can grow
between a day's beginning and its end,
making it seem not like twelve hours but like a gray blanket
weighed down with the blessèd dead,
as if heaven had limits that were about to be reached,
as if a terrible dream I've awaited had pushed its way almost through.
You are, what, a perfect number,
the solution to the equation that was my marriage,
that sadness made me too helpless to work out?
I have to learn which problems can't be solved,
which experiments are too perilous to repeat.
The sky presses on roofs, my head—why, to claim me?
To back time up and whisk me out of it?
No, I can only remain empty as zero for you,
a moon flat and transparent against the blue,
without dark to deepen around me today, like love,
like your arms—*dangerous to live for*?
This is the bare truth: even if my god is not love but my body,
I and all the dark and the world still are alight with my desire
for one more Friday night with you.

Let My Love Fall Over You

A siren's protest sweeps my walls like a beam,
recedes as fast as it swelled,
sounds like someone starved for some ruin
that's not to be found here. My emergency—
that I want someone to tell everything to—
is too trifling for them to rush to. I'm only sick of everything
but the terms you won't utter,
you delicate alert animal
that eats from my hand but won't stay,
your word, your bond elusive
as a stoat or ghost,
frail as paper under my weight,
as grief blowing off the desk in a wind.
Tell me you love me, someone,
let my feeling fall over you
the way the dark falls and falls,
on the black shape down in the street—
bike and hunched rider
scuttling away from me
like a rat with one red eye—
on the migrating bird who sings
for the streetlights it thinks are day.

Learning a Language

For years two skeletons of air
in their air and water coverings,
he the husband, I the wife,
ensconced as we were in our rooms,
homed in on the old familiar cruelties.
Slights glowed like yellow eyes in the dark.
While vows skin made to skin, yours and mine, lover,
have stood at the door for so long now,
like loyal pets, waiting for it to be opened
so they can show us they could run
away from us but do not. They see five
minutes into the future; their language
is knowing what hurt will be wrought
by words wanting to be said, so not saying them;
letting the beast lurking in the skull lie down
and sleep is their language. Speak it to me.

Like a Boat

To the feeling and the truths
caught in the spirit's hold like wild birds I say,
do not take the limits the world imposes
as the soul's limits. Death's dispersing
of a name's gently cohering letters—
is it an end? Into the vast spaces
between the molecules of my flesh
rush the silences. The silence of the phone.
The silence of my mouth
in training not to speak recklessly.
The silence of those to whom I put in
for compliments, attention.
The silence of the secrets the man I love
is compelled to keep.
Each, added to the cargo,
presses me deeper into the stillness,
like a boat leaving its white scar
healing endlessly behind it
on an endless, dying sea.

The Top of the Sky

Though the lid of clouds
that weighed on the city
all month has been lifted,
last night's words
I heard myself saying,
to keep you, still cannot fly
up and away.

A mourning dove
runs across my path,
its bobbing head a blur,
like a feeling with no name.
Desperate love
of foolish women
for foolish men.

We were game-pieces
to each other.
I wanted you
to beat in my body,
my eyes to blink back
the sea inside that poured out.

I'm strolling here
with my shadow,
in the light of lamps,
under a moon
superfluous as desire;
the sky's drawn its starless
blanket back
to show the pulsing circle
it was covering.

Like a player
arriving dressed to compete,
I took a gift for a challenge.
A mind made up
that you unmade,
pulled off a little more each night,
me naked underneath.
All cried out. How will you
love me now?

Under the World

Sounding dessicated and weightless,
feeling filters through the grate
in the street I'm under
onto the platform, around my feet,
a nuisance to be swept up.
These are the tears
the world's trees are shedding.
Everything is sad
about the ending of the world that was,
that never was. Our bones are loose
with nostalgia for delight not taken,
truths kept back, love that should have been.
What is my speech about it
but curled shrunken leaves
milling aimlessly
in the dim still air of a station?

Ghost in the Machine

My home is not empty but free.
I am not subject but queen
of the silence that is not silence
but the machine lying unplugged.
I am warden of the stillness
that I call room—
for reason,
for the feral child loneliness
to be civilized,
for the yawning sheets to be twisted,
for the moving,
your voice moving toward
my ear and away.

What I Can Stand or Count On

I can stand on a boardwalk and count the waves.
I can stand on board a promise or jump out of it,
be a passenger on the Shoot the Chute called New York,
my body a point where the past and the future meet.
I can be one
in the giant shape of shifting points
swooping back and forth like pigeons
fine-tuning ourselves to each other,
shuffling our feet like cards,
everyone sneezing and walking and chewing,
lovers sweetly melded but having to adjust their arms—
what else is there to do? There's laundry, clothes freshened
and worn as leaves. There's standing on the blue earth,
or being in it, or scattered over it like pieces of holy shade or bread.
When I feel the future at the strong back of my body like wind,
while the soft front of my body blends with the past I'm facing,
I'm ready to call a version of myself to my mind that comes like a sheep
or a loyal pet in a well-kept world, like French fries I ordered
and can't wait to eat. Count the pros and cons! Don't open your mouth
for any old story of heaven the devil angel holds out to you. Look at it.
Lick it first. Sleep on it. What dreams I'll have
in that great place! What rides! Ah my darling friends there! My letters!
C, P, T, N, K, all twenty-six of you.
You are the ones that make me stand up,
be counted, laugh! What else is there to do? To think? To think about? To be?

A House of Air

We can either lift ourselves above
the house of what we have said and done to each other
and see the ordered geography of where we live from the air;
or the remembered happiness we play over and over like a beloved song,
the grain of the wood and the flowers on the upholstery
inside the rectangular rooms with their blue beds and their window bars
can imprint their sounds, shapes, colors
into the collective imagination and form its limits.

Would you recognize a room that was not a room,
a house that was an edifice of air,
without angles or human inhabitants?
In a fall prairie, walls of grass
would rise red on either side of you;
you'd have the sky for a ceiling.
On a small mountain lake,
the clouds of what's coming next
would ripple the cattails and overtake you
with their cold and their shade and their weather.

But our shapes are square, our justifications simple,
our time is straight and broken.
We remake the corners in our hearts,
our brains, our politics, and our parks.
A whitewater of chemical emotions
rises around us to engulf us
in notions like lasting love.

Is No More Solid than the

The years have just whispered that the waves washing,
washing, washing the body are not breaking
over me to reassure me that the body
is a coherent thing that can
move through the world
in one piece.
Suddenly it's as if
some servant god had reached
out a delicate white-gloved hand to
deliver this message to me on a salver of sunlight:
even after all this disappearing, after all we've done to
keep, to possess the world, the body
serving up now this, now that
infirmity or condition,
demanding
what are you going
to do NOW? of me is no more
solid than the brainless jellyfish taking over
the oceans. Is no more cohesive or cohering than
what, than the mist that went out into the
warehouse in the dream I had
when I was three, where men
put me on a cement slab and set me on fire
with a match and I died and dispersed. That, it is shown
to me today, was a template for an understanding that I would reach
much later, the later having become now, now that you my
beloved have invasive cancer, that I am mist the waves
on the Sea of Existence let go
into the air to join
the air.

The Day Returning to Me

Where real time comes in is that all this in consciousness is "getting later," changing certain relations in an irreversible manner.

—BENJAMIN WHORF

Caught as we are in our thoughts of time
as a row of cars, a train we ride
whose stations are days, still
somehow our kisses stretch back

behind us like a rope floating on water,
for us to take hold of and be rescued by.

Still, returning to me, you are like a day
bearing the impress of unbroken time,
marked by fighting, washing, joining,
holding every life on earth in you
—mine, the leaves'—like grains of light—there—

that look you have when you see me—
that is how I know my life
is carried in you. The heat in my body
is your mark in me. I am the day
on its way to you out of the darkness
called the night, the touch reaching you
from all those you've missed
but wanted—in my every word to you
every word ever spoken,
changed in the speaking, freshened
in the speaking, like a seasoned

beloved woman rising from her dream of you.

Seeing the Ground

I hope I live to see a day broken as a winter sparrow
with lint in its beak, a day broken open, fear not dormant in it
but gone, a day curled around me under the thick cloud skin
the sky is growing. I will look down at the world on that day, at my feet,
like a daffodil nodding its bonneted head, frantic and obedient,
to survey the grass around it, sessile, yielding cheerily to the wind.
When I lived with people I was like this:
this was me making a nest for everyone,
in the middle of any stupid weather or any storm.
When I began to live alone I began seeing the ground,
telling myself my own stories, kissing myself
goodbye, good morning and good night, yielding like any flower
does to the sun, to the end of the sun, to the snow.

A Way of Thinking and Seeing and Calling

After trying out these ways
to think about my town, my reflection, you—
that living means influences speeding between people;
that loving means replacing the receding image
of my lone self with a word from you—
this is the way I've found.
Even though the face I call "me"
is wrinkled now, the body stiff,
even though the trains
now halt in the dark
and the city containing you is now smothered
in clouds of water and despair.
Even though I have learned that you
call out for me
in your excruciatingly tender,
blatantly silent way,
and Alice Neel and Franz Wright and my father
have cleaned the slate and redrawn the faces,
rewritten the facts—births, deaths—over
and over, begged for a kiss as I have,
just one, in spite of how the remembered dream of,
or night–or fight–with you
is still more vivid than any green leaves
hanging down like millions of quivering legs
from the rows of flowers
that lie along the tops
of the branches of a small viburnum
like all-white spines, in spite of how the bird is invisible
whose worried glorious song
emanates from it,
the plane trees in a line leading me to my office
starting to look like animals

trapped in the bodies of plants by a curse or spell,
their branches entwining
with the bruised sky
like your arms with mine,
even though everything—
a name the same as your name,
the briefly whitened tree,
the man in jeans like yours
passing a buzzing cutter
lightly back and forth
over the shadow the trunk rises from,
tree in its shadow, bird in its tree,
tree and shadow and man in my sight—
everything starts to remind me
of how old I am,
that we are all sick and afraid
of the endlessly somber sky
endlessly leaking away,
of the ailments adding up
to the final one, because
the easy rebellions—too much drinking, lying, careless speech—
give way to the other, real life lifting without ceasing
from the surface of the Atlantic like a thin blue sheath
that floats out and envelops the streetlights—
living by seeing persists.

In the shadow of the Great Lie,
that we will never die,
rights and plans drop
into one's loneliness like stones
into a glass of water.

IN GRATITUDE

I'm deeply grateful to Anita Feldman, who, as my copy editor, read these poems with an acute eye and great intelligence. This book is better because of her.

And my gratitude goes out to my Aux friends, my devoted first readers.

I am also most grateful to Karyn Kloumann. I am delighted and humbled that she has added *Under the World* to the outstanding collection of distinctive art and poetry Nauset Press offers.

... for thanking you ... & for
... much. More & more I ...
... me ... as they ...
... existence ... some ...
... and tenderness and ...
... ... in the ...
... and hopeless ...
... "I am afraid of what the
... your kindness toward me ...
... visit & encourage me in ...
... my work has been ...
Best wishes,

43287809R00039

Made in the USA
Middletown, DE
06 May 2017